The witch of the pine's
Hallowe'en
Conspectvs

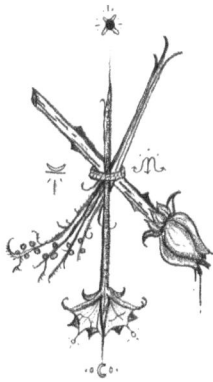

EDITED AND TRANSLATED BY
MICHAEL CONNER

EDITOR'S PREFACE

Dear reader,

As you have somehow come into possession of this book, I am quite certain you must have several questions --- chiefly among them, *"what is this?"* --- which I will get to in a moment. Secondly, and because I myself often ponder this same thing, you must be wondering how it is I came to find --- and no less *translate* --- this text. How did I do it? Why? What authority have I to do such a thing?

Fine questions. Excellent questions.
And the answers are, for the most
part, in keeping with what I hope one
would describe as 'not *completely*
insane'.

If you will indulge me for a few
minutes I will explain --- as best I
can, anyway --- what this is and how
it came to be.

• • •

In the spring of 1997, my parents
bought a modest amount of land in an
unincorporated part of Turtle River,
whichis located somewhere in the south
eastern United States (I cannot

disclose the exact location). They hoped to someday build on this land, or to at least hold on to and sell it at the right time as a bit of a nest egg. The years passed and the land remained undeveloped and undisturbed. Or so we thought.

At some point, several years ago, the Turtle River school district petitioned the county to dump a small number of dilapidated portable schoolroom units deep in the woods. It was an odd, unethical, and wasteful request which was none the less granted, and the "deep woods" into which these units were retired was, in fact, the plot of land my parents had purchased years prior. In an effort to bypass the bureaucratic nightmare of suing the school board to remove the broken and rotting units themselves, I hired a team of construction and demolition professionals to break down the portables and clear the land.

We never got past the initial survey.

• • •

What I am about to tell you is true, implausible though it may seem. Your belief in the otherworldly --- in ghosts and spirits and veils between worlds --- surely plays no small part in why you sought out this book, dear reader, and so I ask you not to veer into cynicism and doubt as we continue deeper into the darkening woods of this recollection; to the irregular, to the supernatural, to the deeply and enrapturingly *odd*.

I met the lead contractor at the head of the path off the main road leading into the woods, quite some distance away from the erratically dumped portables. As we walked closer to inspect --- he wanted to get a sense of how structurally sound they were; how many men and what tools he'd need to properly break down and dispose of the units, and so on --- we were overtaken by a stench that can be best described as incomprehensible. We faltered, stumbled backwards, as if the smell itself had shoved us by the shoulders. Covering my mouth and fighting the urge to vomit, I regained my footing and continued forward, eyes itching and watering. I kicked open the rotting door of the portable and immediately understood why these buildings were disposed of so hastily.

To this day, I am grateful that what I saw did not cause me to descend into absolute madness.

Encompassing nearly the full interior of the unit were groupings of massive, purple pumpkins. Many as large as barrels. Carved into each of them were a series of runic symbols. The 'meat' of the pumpkins underneath the unnatural purple flesh was a sickly, iridescent green. And though every instinct I had told me to turn and leave, to run away and never look back, I was entranced. Mystified.

I told the contractor we'd have to abandon the project, that there were biohazardous materials in the portables, that they would have to remain forever untouched. Still reeling from the stink, he was all too happy to oblige. I never saw him again.

I returned later that night. The green meat of the pumpkins glowed faintly in the darkness. Scrawled along the walls of the portable in a thick, black ink-like substance was a key by which I was able to transcribe the symbols to their latin alphabet counterparts. I made several attempts to transpose the pumpkin carvings to more convenient and less sensory-assaulting forms, but each attempt to copy it to a different medium resulted in some form or another or startling 'interference': attempting to copy the key to paper resulted in the paper igniting and burning to ash; an attempt to photograph the pumpkins resulted in the lens on my phone's camera shattering; a concerted effort to memorize the key resulted in several nights of dreams so intensely disturbing that I cannot bear any

attempt to describe them. What I did,

then, was translate what you are about

to read in real-time, in the portable

by the light of the moon (taking very

shallow breaths!), jotting the

contents down on a notepad as I

believe it is intended to be read, as

quickly as possible.

There were 33 pumpkins in total,

each one represented by a page in this

manuscript. They consist of an

introduction of sorts, thirty-one

entries each corresponding with a day

in the month of October, and one that

read simply, "THE VVITCH OF THE PINE".
I believe this to be the author's
intended *nom de plume.* However, having
studied the document extensively, I am
somewhat unconvinced that this 'Witch
of the Pine' is merely one
individual...

What follows is a manuscript of
curiosities; poems, recipes,
prayer-like meditations, and
presumably useful information on
various creatures and spirits --- and
how to summon them. I have translated
the document as accurately as I

believe possible, and have left intact

both the curious and inconsistent

grammar and syntax as well as several

words that are, simply put,

untranslatable...

Proceed not merely with caution, but

with an open mind and willingness of

spirit.

Michael Conner,

October Eve, 2018

2nd Edition Preface,

or 'A Year of Madness'

I cannot begin to tell you, reader, what a relief it was to publish an initial volume of this manuscript last year, to free myself from the weight of being the only soul aware of its existence, to release the bats in the belfry, as it were.

But I would be lying to you if I said that setting the witch's words out into the world freed me of the strange curse of the Conspectus. Indeed, all that has changed is the

manner in which this deeply perplexing
tome has manifested its presence in my
life.

Over the past year there have
been nights during which I awaken
between midnight and 3a.m., dripping
in a cold sweat, delirious, scribbling
in my notepad. I come-to in the middle
of this fervor, my hand frantically
scratching at the page as though it is
taking orders from a mind other than
my own -- sketching odd images of
rotting pumpkins, ghostly spectres,
and unearthly flowers among other
indescribable things.

It seems as though my work with the Conspectus was not finished, and the witch, or perhaps one of her conspirators, has been taking control of my body to produce the images which I have included in this year's edition of the Halloween Conspectus. I hope that including the images finally satisfies her (*them?*) and that I can now be unbound from this fantastically haunted document.

It is my great fear that these subconscious and otherworldly commands to alter the contents of the

Conspectus will continue forever… but I mustn't dwell on this delusion.

Lastly, reader, as a note of housekeeping for this edition: I have cleaned up what I now believe to have been a few mild translational errors. Additionally, I have included a list of items and ingredients named within the conspectus that are necessary for the enclosed spells and potions, as well as several pages of notes to document your own experiences with the potions and summonings, or perhaps to make a record of any strange

encounters...

   Michael Conner,

   Fall 2019

Items & Ingredients

various spells, potions, and rituals found within the
Conspectus may require the following elements:

- Unscented candles
- Bundle of dried mugwort
- Sun-cleansed salt
- Spiced wine
- Lemons (or seasonal "tarted" fruit)
- Ginger
- Oats or nuts, milked
- Honey
- Turmeric
- Distilled spring water
- Black licorice root
- Fulvic acid
- Hibiscus oil
- "Golden Root" (Rhodiola), crushed
- 2 small wall mirrors
- Dried *solanaceae* (flowers within the *Nightshade* family -- not further specified)
- Lavender oil
- Apple cider

- Pumpernickel
- Sweet preserves
- Twine
- Absinthe [though you are free to ferment your own concoction of star pod, wormwood, etc., the end result is absinthe - of which pre-made will surely suffice...]

For those who wish to undergo the process of becoming a werewolf:
I cannot knowingly consent to a course of action that will surely kill those who attempt it, thus I will not list the necessary elements. You are on your own!

The
Hallowe'en Conspectvs

ALL YE SHALL FIND HEREIN IS TO BE:
Read aloud,
incanted,
prepared & consumed,
OR otherwise instructed ---
**BY FLAME OF THE CANDLE IN THE HOUR
OF OWL'S LIGHT**

Beginning: FIRST OF OCTOBER
Concluding: HALLOWE'EN

∞

THE DOXONOCTURNE

Incant at first light of moon, October 1
stand centre in the room whence thy energy radiates
strongest
cleanse by burning of dried Mugwort
salt all entry points
imbibe of spiced wine
EXTINGUISH ALL LIGHT

Incant the following:

Come thou light of owl,
Come thou beam of moon.
As daylight ever-dwindles
marked by summer's death in June.

May whispers impart wisdom,
may shadow steel my sight.
May the darkness that resides within
be balanced by the night.

As the veil begins to lower may we be protected:

By no hex shall I be bound.
No troll shall I let confound.
May there be no lurking pukwudgies
in the places where I roam.
May no goblins, ghouls, or wirry-carles
follow me back home.

The realms' convergence nigh,
The Hallowed Eve is coming soon!
May I find light and guidance
in the secrets of the Moon.

ODE TO THE LOWER'D VEIL

*A poem to solidify thy mind against the tricks of wiley
sprites and spectres*

Couldst thou believe thine eye
If like black flame flickering in the sky
thirteen felines upon their brooms went soaring by?
If like the sail of a ship,
like the crack of a whip
The Goblin King's cape
caught the wind from on high?

Wouldst thou believe thine eye
If tumbling out of the darkening pine
A skeleton holding his whistling head you did spy?
If out of the night
came the curious sight
Of a flurry of bats of unusual size?

Shouldst thou believe thine eye
If masked and hooded passers-by
Skipped along by lantern light laughing 'neath their
          guise?
If at thirteenth hour death
bloomed like a flower
And up from their slumber the dead did arise?

Believe it so!
Believe it seen!
The veil shall lower on the Eve!

If what ye see
Should make ye shout
Close thy eyes or pluck them out!
For spectral visions shall portend
the coming HALLOWE'EN!

THE WITCH'S WOMB

Although the lore is lost to time,
the Jack-o-lantern is, in fact,
A snickering, cackling *memorandum*
Of the witch's womb

A barren thing of wax and flies,
A rotted, burning blight;
No more a place of fruited seed--
A cold and empty tomb

'tis now the way that it must be--
The price the witch has paid
To return once more thru lower'd veil
Descending on her broom

And though the witch cannot bear fruit
A mother's heart she has
She hears the broken and distraught
And o'er their house she looms

And if you should afflict your young
November 1st reveals:
Your Jack-o-lantern smashed to bits,
Your child's empty room!

October 4
A PRACTICAL POTION

To fortify oneself from the mischief & malice of trickster spirits

PREPARATION:

- Juice of a tarted fruit (lemon, clementine, catseye root) - one beldam's ladle
- Dust of ginger
- Milk extracted of nut or oat - one fair potion's bottle
- Tumeric - three crow's beaks
- Bee's nectar - ONE drop
    - THOU MUST BE GRANTED THE BEE'S PERMISSION TO EXTRACT HER NECTAR OR THE POTION WILL SOUR

Stir vigorously, do not allow to set
And upon this elixir you may bet!

***If thou art being stalked or seduced by the vampyr, mix cider of fresh apple, garlic, and vinegar to the mixture and consume by light of the sun thrice daily to render thy blood unappetizing.

PURPLE, ORANGE, BLACK, & GREEN

*Cloak thyself in the COLOURS OF THE EVE to roam
freely amongst the goblins & ghosts*

Purple, orange, black, and green--
The spectral spectrum of HALLOWE'EN;

Green is for the glowing guts of graveyard ghouls;
Garish goblins gorging on grandly growing gourds;
Ghosts gathering in the gloam and roaming through
the glen.

Purple is for poison potions, pentagrams, and
people-eaters;
Putrid pumpkins that propagate in playgrounds,
parks, and pastures;
Silent psychics petrified by poltergeist possession.

Orange is for owls oscillating in the overgrowth;
The opaque orb of the ominous oracle;
The otherworldly ombré of October overcast

Black is for bats, basilisk blood, and burnt bones;The
beady, beckoning eyes of the Beast from the Beyond;
The billowing bloom of the bog-witch's boiling broth

Purple, orange, black, and green--
Heed the colors of HALLOWE'EN!

TO SPOT A TWI-LITE SPIRIT

CHILDREN! You must read this page in private! Away from the prying eyes of dreadful parents. They seek, as with all Good things, to EXPLOIT the magic of the Twi-lite Spirits! Secrets hitherto unknown to children follow these words:

Twi-lite spirits are all around! As the VEIL lowers they are most mischievous, aye! But greet them with a wink and a knowing nod and good fortune will befall ye on HALLOWE'EN!

The Twi-lite Spirits present as such:

1. A busy bee circling a sprig of lavender in sets of widdershins three!

2. A conspicuous cat with a knowing glance who appears before you and flicks her tail like so:
   left, left, right, left
   left , right, right, left
   Upward curl

3. A spider in the corner of your room at night who has disappeared by light of morn. (He takes his leave at 3:31 a.m. but you mustn't follow him! Leave him be and greet him as told above!)

The mischievous good fortune of the Twi-lite Spirit may be paid in many forms. Often, it is as a great embarrassment befalling one who has met you with an unkind heart. But BEWARE! For those whom YOU have met with an unkind heart may too receive the good fortune of the TWI-LITE SPIRITS!

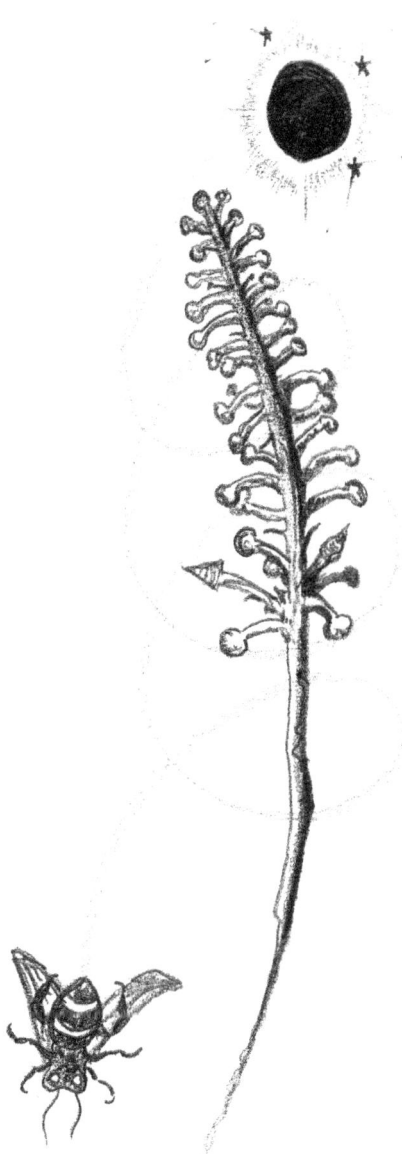

LAVENDER;
BEE;
WIDER JINS III

THE SINGING SKELETON

A boy of thirteen harvests
went out on HALLOWE'EN.
Then home he went a-counting
All the treats that he had gleaned.
All fat on cakes and candies,
his belly was a-wringing.
When just outside his window,
He saw a skeleton singing:

HA HA! -- HO HO! -- HEE HEE!
AS I AM YOU TOO SHALL BE!
HA HA! -- HO HO! -- HEE HEE!

Thirteen harvests, cycles two,
the little boy had grown.
And then indeed, on HALLOWE'EN,
out went a son -- his own!
And as he watched him down the lane,
The autumn wind a-stinging,
Beside him, a horrific fright--
The skeleton was singing:

HA HA! -- HO HO! -- HEE HEE!
AS I AM YOU SOON SHALL BE!
HA HA! -- HO HO! -- HEE HEE!

Many harvest after this, the father's time was nigh.
And as such his family gathered 'round to say
goodbye.
"Now heed my final words," the father said, a smile
springing.
His flesh began to fade away, and lo! he was
a-singing:

HA HA! -- HO HO! -- HEE HEE!
AS I AM YOU TOO SHALL BE!
HA HA! -- HO HO! -- HEE HEE!

BEWARE THE WRATHFUL LORDESS OF THE WOOD

Beware the wrathful lordess of the wood!
She be fox!
She be crow!
She be doe!
She does not stalk by pallor of moon
For she circles your camp by light of day
Black eyes absorbing the warmth of the sun
WOE TO THE MORTAL MAN WHOSE LEADEN
FOOT CRACKS TREEFALL IN HER PATH
greet her by tongue familial and mercy may befall ye

BO DESS ESS AH SEM[1]

---

[1] I am at a total loss for a translation here. Night after night, bleary-eyed at 3 a.m., I found myself scouring every available resource for every available dialect of Celtic, Gaelic, Latin (the usual suspects); Aramaic, Hebrew...nothing. Nothing human, anyway. I think there may be a chance that the witch has spelled this "greeting" phonetically since proper pronunciation seems of extreme importance. But again, that's all it is - a guess... -M.C.

Say it once!
Only once!
She hath no time for your clacking tongue,
For what thou hast said she hath heard
She hath seen the death and destruction what thou
hath wrought
SHE IS ANGRY

BO DESS ESS AH SEM

BATSKIN, CATSKIN, RATSKIN

BE YE BATSKIN, CATSKIN, or RATSKIN?

Beware the ratskin - black of blood and pale of skin
He is quick to anger -- his wits be thin
But the kin of the cat devours the rat!
Even of keel - she goes titt for tatt
And the bat! The bat! Kin of the bat!
In darkest of night can see where you're at
An empath -- true and fair!
      (The cat will meet you halfway there)
But the compassion of the rat is as thin as a hair!

BEWARE! BEWARE!
For your kin is not fixed
And the noblest cat can shrink into a rat
With the speed of a devilish black mage's trick
Yet the sewer-bound rat can align with the bat
If a solicitous path he doth pick

To swoop with the bat your sense must be keen
Indeed you must see what has thus gone unseen
And to slink with the cat is a steadfast affair
With virtuous temperament otherwise rare
The rat does not care! The rat does not care!
      (And it cannot be said that he's just unaware)

So be careful before you go slinking and swooping
and creeping and crawling out into the night
For the cats and the rats and the bats are all waiting
To see what alignment your heart deemeth right!

LETTER FROM A GARDEN'S GHOST

Whilst conjuring under the eye of the cat's moon, the
wayward spirit beseeched me:
"witch, hear my cries! Find my love and tell them this which
I shall dictate."
The words of the spirit follow:

Dearest,
Though I am departed, know I have not gone from
you
In the particles that stir in the beams of morning
light -- I am there
In the sturdy grain of creaking beams -- I am there
I long for you to see me
I long for you to feel me
But I know that in your material state you cannot
And I know no measure of time
Eternity is an endless dusk

With regret I must confess that my sadness has
spoiled and sprouted into rage

My screams slam the kitchen cabinets
Shattering the panes
splintering the wood

The objects of my affection for you
Which you have kept in place
And free of dust
I push them off the table
I hurl them into the wall

The fear in which you cower and cry out is my own
doing -- For this I must repent

And so I have taken refuge in the sanctuary of your
garden
Where I learn to be like the periwinkles and peonies
that rustle in the breeze
cooling your face;
Like the humble and diligent butterflies and bees
Busy with their nectar
They greet me as they go about their day
It is here I will remain
And together we shall watch your flowers blossom
and bloom
And when they wither and die
As they surely will
I will caress you as the breeze
And we will be one season closer to reunion

TO SPOT A WITCH

FOOL!
Thou can spot a witch only if she wishest to be seen!
    (and she be not haggard or warted or green)

There is but one truth of the witch I shall give:
    Even in death, she continues to live!

PARABLE OF THE MAD DOCTOR

If ye be mortal, heed these words: it is against the divine wish to resist death, for where there is life, death MUST FOLLOW! Be not afraid -- for the warmth of the sun beams down for thee in life, and the shadowveil of moon blossoms for thee in death.

A mad and brilliant doctor, it is said, brought a cadaver of stolen limbs and skin and eyes to life in his laboratory.

The creature (for it could not be called "man") was fearsome and large and wept for its own existence.

And when the townspeople came upon the doctor's laboratory with torches and pitchforks and axes in hand, he was not surprised.

Magnanimously, he greeted them:

"I understand you are confused and afraid," he said to the crowd. "But there is nothing to fear, for I have conquered death! I simply cannot allow you to take the head of my creature. He must live!"

"We know what you've done," said a man of the crowd. "But it is not your creature's head we've come to claim...

It is *yours!*"

THE AUTUMN CHILD

A requiem for the misunderstood Children of October

The autumn child is the scattering of dried leaves,
and billowing plume of violet smoke arising in the
dead wood,
heralding the season & the shrinking light of day.

The autumn child is the first firefly, the first cricket
embracing the perfect shade of twi-lite;
the still air of the waking moon.

The autumn child is the 13th black cat sitting under a
ladder
admiring her reflection in the shards of a mirror;
Candle wax dripping onto velvet.

The autumn child is the distant laughter that
concerns watchful parents;
The richochetting snap of twigs,
The sudden wisp of breeze.

The autumn child sits contented in the corner of the
room,
speaking the tongue of the beetles and worms,
exchanging secrets of the earth.

A PECULIAR POTION

To ready thy mind for communication with those whom beyond the veil preside

PREPARATION:

- one fair potion's bottle of undisturbed water
- Black licorice root, ground
- Fulvic acid over which the blessing of gratitude hath been performed
- Essence of hibiscus
- three faerie's bundles of Golden Root, crushed
- Bring to a boil in thy cauldron or iron vessel

Transfer thy mixture into the ceremonial cup and bring to the lips slowly...

October 15,
or upon the new moon
THE BLACK MOON INCANTATION

To be incanted once darkness has descended upon middle
Oktobernacht
The power of this incantation increases when amplified by
Many Voices.
By light of the fire in open field,
Shroud thyself in black,
And become like the night

Incant the following:

Black moon
Black moon
World must turn, All must decay

Black moon
Black moon
Show us now another way

Black moon
Black moon
Return from death which shall subsume

Black moon
Black moon
Tonight that I might see

Black moon
Black moon
Like you we seek to be

Black moon
Black moon

Black moon
Black moon

Thou may repeat THE DOXONOCTURNE at this
time to further solidify thy protection.

The Veil is now halfway lowered.

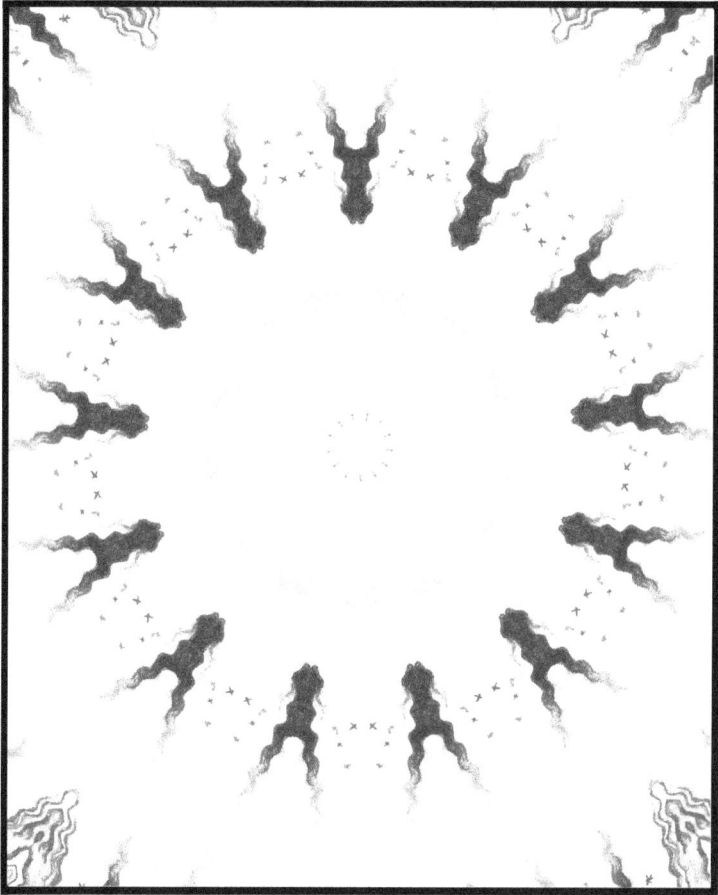

TO REVEAL THE FAERIE'S LIGHT

All which takes breath does so in the light of a faerie.
The faerie may be drawn to one, or as such as one may
attract the faerie.

TO REVEAL THE FAERIE'S LIGHT - Look steadfast
upon the eyes of the one whose light you seek. Keep
still your eye in such a way as it begins to sting but
do not blink. Thy vision may gloss and haze but stay
true in thy sight of the eyes before you and you may
see a light of fantastical color emerge like shadow
from the head or extremities. DO NOT LOOK
DIRECTLY upon the light or it shall vanish. Heed
the color of the faerie's light

GREEN: This individual is in the light of the garden
faerie and as such is balanced in heart and mind

BLUE: This individual is in the light of the faerie of
skies who bestows great healing

VIOLET: This individual is in the light of the night
faerie and is thus possessed of keen intuition

RED OR **BLACK**: BEWARE for this is NOT the light of the faerie, but of a cursed parvos daemon who conjures and feasts on ill thoughts. This individual must be met with kindness and healing to DRIVE OUT the daemon.

Faeries and as such daemons are keener of power as HALLOWE'EN approaches!

<u>WITCHSPIT</u>

*In memoriam of witching spirits robbed of Earthly life
by the ignorance and hatred of man*

Bound by rope,
set upon the pyre
I laugh at your fervor
I laugh at your flames
Convicted:
"loose with devil's tongue"
I will not give my sisters' names

Pious men
art vile in shadow!
I welcome your rancor
I welcome your hate
Ignited!
Thus ye think me done
Fools! I am loosed of my temporal state!

Submerged in light,
returned to dust
Free of the body
In Wester I blow
declarest "dead!"
But I remain:

The bountiful harvest of what ye have sown

Look now! See!
I return for thy end
Ye dullards, ye villains, fanatics, and knaves
Behold--
      Transfiguration!
I dance on the moon
I spit on your graves

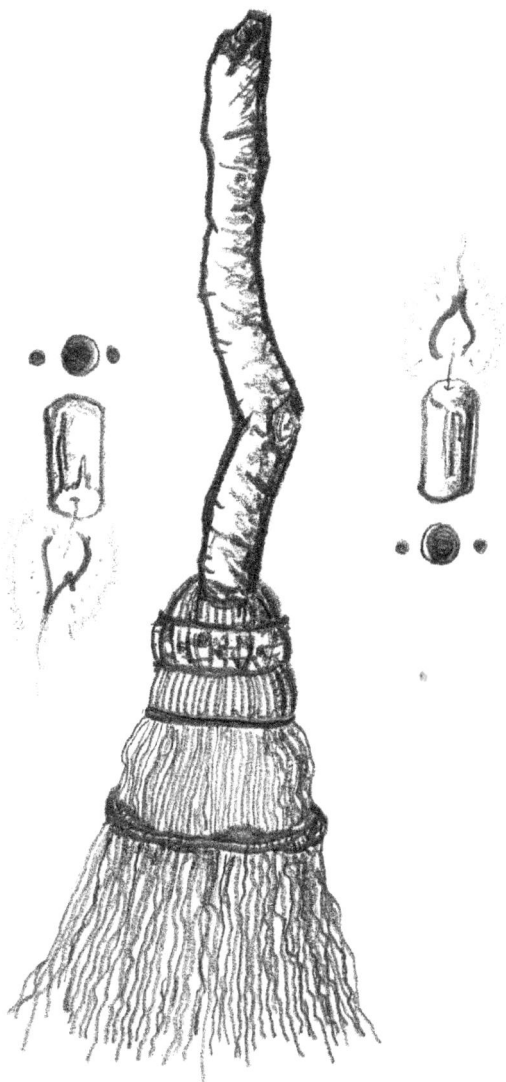

TO SUMMON THE GHOST WHO GOES
BETWEEN WALLS

The Ghost Who Goes Between Walls hears all, sees all
Should you pine for knowledge unattainable, you may wish
to attempt the summoning

PREPARATION:

In a square and unadorned room, hang two mirrors
facing each other on opposite walls.
On the center wall, hang a portrait of the one whose
secrets you wish to have revealed.
On a small table in the center of the room, present
an offering of dried *Solanaceae* and lavender oil.

Incant the following:

Ghost who goes between the walls,
Answer now this mortal call
I seek a knowledge here unknown
Reveal to me your secrets all

The Ghost Who Goes Between Walls is famously persnickety. Should they agree to bestow knowledge upon you, the scent of lavender will fill the room and the knowledge you seek you shall have. In turn, the Ghost Who Goes Between Walls is now privy to your deepest and innermost secrets, and The Ghost may be called upon by others who wish to know that which lurks in the shadows of your being.

ODE TO THE DEVIL DOG

A devil dog makes a most curious companion--
      (Ask Piamon or Bifrons or Shax or Dantalian)
A true and obedient four-legged friend
      (Though the damned and the tortured may
      somewhat contend)

He makes quick work of a good many bones--
      (His favorites are femurs, coccyges, and toes)
With tail wagging gaily and eyes glowing red
      (His growl shakes the ground and unsettles
      the dead)

Oh devil dog, devil dog - faithful indeed
      (Keep ten paces back when it's his time to
      feed!)

TO FEED THE DEAD

*As the veil ever lowers, so the dead begin to roam.
With the following appease them should they wander to thy
home.*

Prepare a setting by light from three candles,
unscented (*Do not* use floral scents) and afix the
following:

- 1 cup (per spirit) of lukewarm apple cider in a
  stemmed glass
- 1 piece (per spirit) of darkened pumpernickel
  coated heavily with sweet preserves
  - DO NOT set any utensils
- Allow the candles to burn completely OR for
  seventeen minutes, whichever shall first
  occur.
    Incant the following:

SPIRITS ALL, BEHOLD
IN LIFE I HONOR DEATH

- Consume that which has been prepared

*This will appease the dead and protect thee from
malevolence*

THE WITCH'S WEEDS

These be the weeds most precious and practical to witching.
Take ye note of the applications of the witch's weeds!

DATURA STRAMONIUM - The Thorn-Apple.
Known to man as "Jimsonweed". The prickly fruit is
well served to war-mongering hordes of men, who
shall find themselves delirious, dumbfounded, and
stripped nude in the black woods where witches be
known to roam...

ATROPA BELLADONNA - The Night's Shade. Her
essence used in spare amount shall relieve ye from
pain of body and mind; her essence used in generous
amount shall relieve ye from pain of a deceitful
man...

HYOSCYAMUS - Hen's Bane. Used in good favour
shall reduce shakings, lesser possessions, and fits of
nightwalking. Seeds may be planted to mark
ceremonial buryings. When taken in a witch's dose it
shall ready thee to project thy spirit beyond the veil.

MANDRAGORA OFFICINARUM - The Man-Drake. The Mother's oil. If thou Mandragora is met with kindness, fed with spoonfuls of sweetmilk, it shall aid thee in matters of love and fertility, and grant thee an agreeable labouring. In manifestation of spirits into the living side of the Veil, powder of the Man-Drake is to be mixed with powder of *Origanum dictamnus* and bound with resin.

CONIUM MACULATUM - The Winter's Fern. The Mark of Cain. Hemlock. May be used to paralyze the body, and indeed - if ye coven be of enough spiritual fortitude - is instrumental to the incantation of halting time itself.

Fig. XIII

~~Datura Atropis~~

THE Night Bloom
distills the heart
... ...
... offering

THE GOBBYLIN SONG

The juanty song favored by rambunctious witches and warlocks known as 'The Gobbylin Song' is meant to incite the anger of goblins, for they are dumb and ill-tempered. Though the tune is lost to time, it is said to have sounded not unlike a raucous sea-shanty.

Mortals be forewarned - goblins are known to swarm upon those who sing this song too loudly in the deep of the woods in the dead of the night as HALLOWE'EN approaches...

The gobbylin hobs
The gobbylin nobs
The gobbylin is a lawless slob
The gobbylin hocks
The gobbylin nocks
The gobbylin steals and eats your socks
Gobbylins fair, and gobbylins mild--
NO SUCH THING -- all gobbylins are wild!

THE SPIDERING FLOWER

Deep in a forest unblemished by man
Where the nightshade and hen's bane
grow hand in hand
There lies a great flower that never has bloomed
(and if it should blossom then mankind is doomed)
This flower is not like the others you know,
Inside it a most wicked trick has been sewn
For should it be mowed down or trampled aside,
10 trillion spiders lay waiting inside!
Destructors and razers and trespassers all,
The Spidering Flower will answer this call:

*up the walls, through the cracks
in your hair, up your back
Spiders pouring from the hearth
Spiders cover up the earth
In your ears, in you brain
Is where the spiders' eggs are laid
In your mouth, in your eyes
spiders small and large in size
You cannot run, you cannot hide
Spider webs fill up the sky
Spider flower, spider flower
Bloom and bring the final hour*

A PERPLEXING POTION

To do what thou wilt

UNTO THE FIRE'D CAULDRON:

Breath of Afrit, hair of Alfar
Spot of Crocotta, scale of Namtar
Basilisk fang & Hircocervus hoof
Thy best imitation of Cynocephaly's woof!

Cyclops tear, Caladrius feather
blood of lapwing claimed in fair weather
seed of the apple, wisp o' the will
Ink from the well of the soothsayer's quill

Stir about and boil the mixture
BEHOLD!
This shall yield thee the Great Witch's elixir

SAITH THE WITCH: THIS SHALL DO YE GOOD!
HA! HA!

TO BECOME A WEREWOLF

Thou cannot simply become a werewolf, for the werewolf is a malevolent spirit which must bind with the soul of a mortal in order to materially cross the Veil. If thou wishest (beyond reason!) to submit to the spectral parasite which the werewolf be, heed the following:

There exists a particular mountain within a range which is visible only when the moon is full and the veil is no less than ⅓ lowered. It shall appear upon the following coordinates:

$$47^* 13'28" \text{ N}$$
$$113^* 47'59" \text{ W}$$

At the zenith of the mountain, there shall appear an iron cauldron. If the cauldron boils and smokes, thou may proceed. It will neither boil nor smoke if thou hast failed to meet its demands. It demands thus:

- thou must make thy intention known before the mountain. Speak it so to the pines. If thou art received kindly, the fog shall part.

- Thou must shed all garments before climbing. The werewolf requires raw flesh with which to bind itself.

- Thou must abstain from contact with mortal beings for no less than 13 hours prior to the climb.

If the cauldon gives signal to proceed, thou art to submit the following offerings into the boiling mixture:
- 13 fresh drops of thy blood
- The knife with which the cut was made
- The skin of a dog
- Absinthe
- Opium
- Myrrh

If thou hast succeeded thus far, the cauldron shall emit a stark white smoke thou art to inhale deeply. The binding shall begin. The process shall involve great torment [...][2]
And though thou shall taste of immortality, with it comes unceasing lust for blood and chaos at the sight of the full moon.

May mercy come to whosoever shall attempt the binding.

---

[2] This section - perhaps detailing the "great torment" - has been scratched out and rendered illegible. -M.C.

October 26
TO MAKE A GATHERING GROUND FOR WISTFUL SPIRITS

This is the place you have seen in dreams.

Gather your linens, twine, and pins. Listen to your true sense, let it lead you to the place in the woods which is far from the living man, the place deemed safe and holy by the birds and reptiles. Here you will find the babbling water which passes undisturbed. Along the graceful path the sun shines in beams through the cover of trees on the smooth rocks and warm dirt. Here is where you will find the branches. String up your twine in great swooping pivots from branch to branch. Hang your linens. They will begin to sway in time to the music of the woods. You needn't hide or retreat. Make yourself known. Be still. The spirits will gather, darting and swinging about within and around the linens, playing like children. Listen for their voices in the chirping and buzzing, in the flowing of the water. Listen for their whispers. Great secrets of that which awaits beyond may be revealed to those who are patient.

THE BLACK CAT

Black Cat emerges like shadow, like fog
Comes to bear witness to All Hallow's Eve
See now the creatures who clatter and clog
Even more graceless than she could conceive

Out in the distance the skeleton clangs,
Head rolling 'round with a bang and thud
Even the vampire's slender white fangs
Put to poor use -- for they suck *human* blood!

She pays no mind to the goblins and trolls
For little is worse than clumsy green fools
Save for the werewolf -- pathetic poor soul
Truly a fright to see how much he drools!

Black Cat is vapor among the night sky
Rolling her eyes as the ghosts clamber by

A PRACTICAL GUIDE TO TRICK-OR-TREATERS

To those who may wish to keep indoors during
HALLOWE'EN take heed,
For trick-or-treaters may not be what they seem...

- Be wary of guising youngsters in groups of 6,
  For one amongst them is Master of Tricks

- Give extra treats to those in home-made
  disguise,
  For they know the magic words that make the
  dead come alive!

- To those who would assume the guise of
  creatures of the night
  Be certain as they approach your home that
  your candles are alight...

- Be kind to Trick-or-Treaters one and all,
  Lest you be aggrieved by mischievous spirits
  next Fall!

October 29

TO SUMMON [?????][3]

Gather at dusk in circles of three
Open outstretched arms to me
Lend me voice with tongue and tooth
Join together hand and hoof
And gladly I shall appear to thee

---

[3] Unlike the other 'how to' entries found in the Conspectus, this one does not include instructions, ingredients, or tasks relating to any sort of preparation. The entry itself seems to have been dictated to whomever hastily wrote the words. Furthermore, the word or name of that which is meant to be summoned is displayed as a symbol unrepeated anywhere else in the entries and thus I cannot translate it. I do not wish to guess as to who (or what) this creature may be... -M.C.

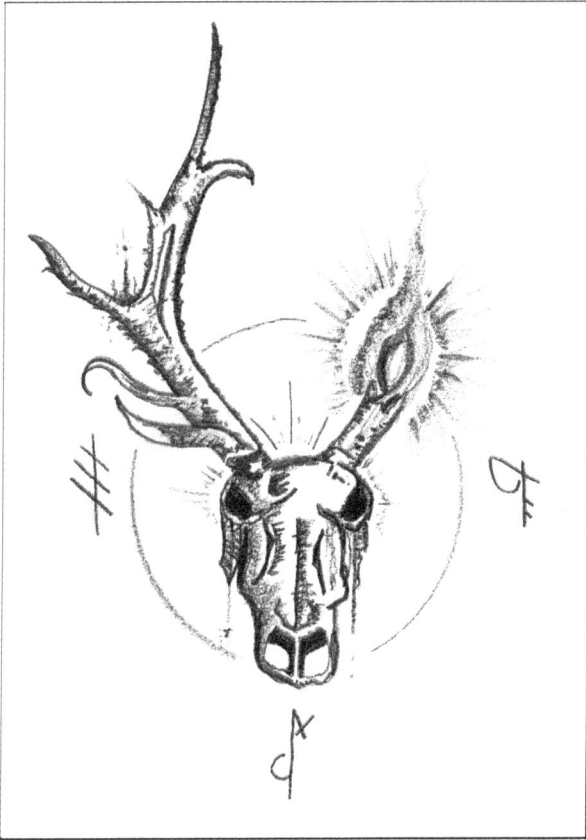

TO IMBIBE WITH ROAMING SPIRITS

This night is the night when the Veil is lowest before
dematerializing on HALLOWE'EN
As such, spirits have begun to gather in great number
Restless
Awaiting the great Night!

PREPARATION:

Ready the fermented drink which contains the
following:

- Star pod
- Wormwood
- Black licorice
- Hyssop
- Lemon
- Angelica root

Transfer the mixture into a black vessel which
cannot be penetrated by the light
Form an outer circle of salt and twine 12 paces wide
Form an inner circle of ash and twine 3 paces wide

Thou needn't summon the spirits.
They are already present.

Keep centre of the inner circle lest thou be vulnerable to the
tricks of the spirits
Take of the drink from the black vessel upon each line of the
following
incant:

Spirits of cold black air
SUAIMHNEAS!
Spirits that haunt and despair
SUAIMHNEAS!
Spirits that gather and grow
SUAIMHNEAS!
Spirits whose presence shall soon be known
SUAIMHNEAS!

With this, thou hast beseeched kindness from those
which roam the beyond.
Thou should not expect a reply...

Thou hast been heard.

HALLOWE'EN

The night has come,
the moon is high
The twi-light shadow fills the sky
The realms converge,
The veil is down
Spirits gather all around!

Before you go into the night
Burn this poem by lantern light--
The plume of smoke shall give you guise!

TAKE TO THE STREETS!
TAKE TO THE SKIES!

ARISE!

ARISE!

ARISE!

ARISE!

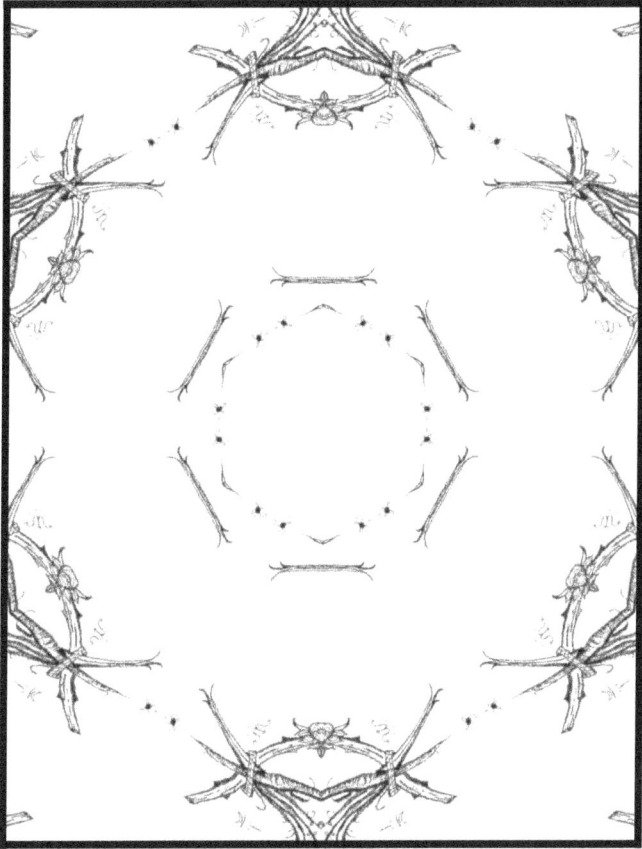

POST-SCRIPT

Dear reader,

If you have made your way through
the Conspectus --- following accurately
its whims and instructions --- and
remain foundationally unmoved in spirit,
then your soul is of stronger reserve
than mine. I find myself at its mercy on
a sensory level throughout the year: a
faint whiff of lavender, the taste of a
vampire-repelling tonic, a spider
darting up the wall in the corner of my
vision. Each year as October draws near
these sensations increase in intensity,
and the otherworldly images within begin
to commandeer my dreams --- black cats

on brooms, whistling skeletons, phantom mountain ranges shrouded in fog. I begin to feel supernaturally drawn to the Conspectus, as though it is calling out to me, beckoning for its mysterious power to once again be set upon the mortal world for thirty-one magical and mischievous days. If you experience a similar feeling, I hope you will allow this copy of the text to be your guide through the yearly lowering of the Veil --- from now until we step beyond this side of it.

Eternally yours in Halloween spirit,

Michael Conner
Halloween 2021, ∞

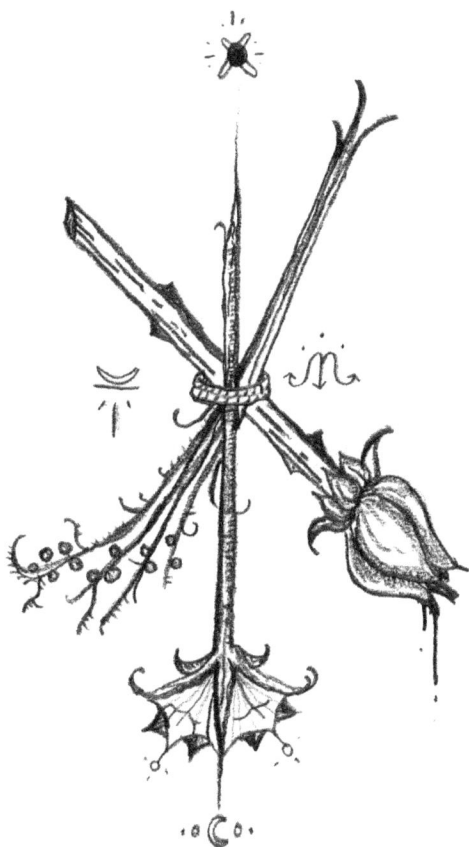

notes

notes

notes

notes

www.ingramcontent.com/pod-product-compliance
Lightning Source LLC
Chambersburg PA
CBHW021625270326
41931CB00008B/866